This Ladybird book
belongs to

....

LADYBIRD BOOKS

UK | USA | Canada | Ireland | Australia
India | New Zealand | South Africa

Ladybird Books is part of the Penguin Random House group of companies
whose addresses can be found at global.penguinrandomhouse.com.
www.penguin.co.uk   www.puffin.co.uk   www.ladybird.co.uk

First published 2023
001
Written by Ashley Harris Whaley
Illustrated by Ananya Rao-Middleton with Hannah Wood
Text and illustrations copyright © Ladybird Books Ltd, 2023
Printed in Italy

The authorized representative in the EEA is Penguin Random House Ireland,
Morrison Chambers, 32 Nassau Street, Dublin D02 YH68

A CIP catalogue record for this book is available from the British Library
ISBN: 978–0–241–57311–2

All correspondence to:
Ladybird Books, Penguin Random House Children's
One Embassy Gardens, 8 Viaduct Gardens
London SW11 7BW

I AM
YOU ARE

Written by
Ashley Harris Whaley

Illustrated by
Ananya Rao-Middleton

We are all different.

Diversity means we are all different.

There are more than eight billion people on Earth!

More than one billion people on Earth are disabled.

Disability is a part of human diversity.

All kinds of people have disabilities.

Disabled people can be kids or grown-ups . . .

siblings or grandparents . . .

WE ALL . . .
LOOK DIFFERENT.
BELIEVE DIFFERENT THINGS.
THINK DIFFERENTLY.
LEARN DIFFERENTLY.
MOVE DIFFERENTLY.

teachers or doctors . . .

artists or astronauts . . .

scientists, truck drivers, authors or athletes.

Disabled people are all of these things and more.
A disabled person can be anyone.

As there are so many disabled people in the world,
it is important that we learn how to talk about disability.

What is disability?

Disability is a word that means there are certain things a person's body or brain can't do.

People with disabilities adapt to do things in ways that may look different but work for them. When you **adapt**, you must make changes to suit you and your needs.

"I sit down to put on my clothes."

"I learned to open a jar with one hand."

"I can hold a paintbrush with my foot."

"I wear sunglasses when lights are too bright."

You should be proud of what you can do, and you should never feel bad about what you can't do.

People are disabled for different reasons.

Some people are born disabled, and that is the life they know. You might be born blind, or autistic, or with cerebral palsy. If you are born disabled, disability is just your everyday life.

"I was born without the sense of sight."

"I became sick, and now I need to spend more time resting in my bed."

Others become disabled when they are injured or sick. You might fall or have an accident that means you need to use a wheelchair from that point on. You might get sick and need more care and rest than you used to. You will learn a new way to live in the world, and disability will become your everyday life, too.

There is no reason to be uncomfortable around people with disabilities. Being disabled is not sad, tragic or something to fear. It is simply the way some people are.

DISABILITY CAN BE SOMETHING TO BE PROUD OF!

Some people have disabilities you CAN see.

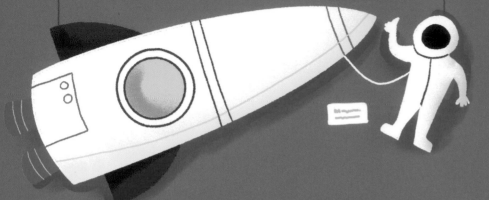

A person might walk differently, have a facial difference, have a limb difference or have a skin condition.

A person might have a feeding tube under their clothing, or they might tire easily. They might deal with long-lasting pain that we can't see.

You might use a wheelchair to get around, a cane to walk, glasses to see or hearing aids to hear. Wheelchairs, crutches, prosthetics and other aids offer their users freedom!

If a person has a learning disability or difficulty, it means they learn differently. To someone with dyslexia, letters look different and reading is difficult. Dyscalculia makes numbers confusing.

MUSEUM ROOM 09

Some people have disabilities you CAN'T see.

People communicate in all sorts of different ways. Not everyone communicates by speaking out loud. We can also communicate using sign language, written communication or electronic devices. All communication is valid and should be respected.

People can think, feel or experience things differently. If someone is **neurodivergent**, their brain works in a unique way.

DO YOU HAVE A DISABILITY? IS ANYONE YOU KNOW DISABLED?

If you stim, you might move your body in certain ways or make sounds to express and manage your emotions. You might tap your foot, or flap your hands when you are happy. Stimming is not something to laugh at or be alarmed by. Stimming is a form of self-expression and a way of communicating.

Every brain is a beautiful brain – and there is no such thing as normal, anyway!

Disability is diverse.

There are millions of disabled people in the world. The disability community is large, and it is diverse.

Disabled people don't all act the same way, learn the same way, move the same way or think the same way.

Two people with the same kind of disability can be affected in different ways.

Some neurodivergent people wear headphones for sound control, others don't; some have highly developed vocabularies while others do not use spoken language.

Some people have disabilities that are **dynamic**. This means that they change from one day to the next. If you have dysautonomia, you might feel like walking one day, but the next day you might have a fast-beating heart and need to use your wheelchair.

Other people have disabilities that stay very much the same from day to day. If you have a learning disability, the support you require is unlikely to change from week to week. If you have cerebral palsy, the way you walk feels the same each day.

People with disabilities have a lot of different experiences and perspectives to share.

What is ableism?

Ableism means that people with disabilities are treated differently, poorly or unfairly because they are disabled – and for no other reason. It also means that people without disabilities are treated more kindly and fairly because they are **not** disabled.

ABLEISM IS ALL AROUND US.

It shows up in unkind words.

It shows up in spaces that are not accessible, like buildings without ramps or videos without subtitles.

It shows up in biases, which are unfair assumptions we make about others.

ABLEISM IS FOUND EVERYWHERE IN OUR WORLD AND OUR SOCIETIES.

ABLEISM IS WRONG.

Making someone feel insignificant because of their disability is wrong.

It is **not OK** for anyone to think that they are better than a disabled person.

It is **not OK** to treat another person unfairly or poorly, just because they have a disability.

Let's not make assumptions about people with disabilities.

Let's **not** assume someone can't play because they have a prosthetic arm or leg.

Let's **not** assume someone isn't smart because their brain works in different ways.

Let's **not** assume someone can't make art because they have trouble seeing.

Let's **not** assume someone can't dance because they are a wheelchair user.

The world can be a tricky place.

The world around us isn't always **accessible**. It was not designed with disabled people in mind.

The world around us isn't always **inclusive**. It often doesn't welcome people with disabilities or allow them to feel like they belong.

For many years, disabled people were not expected or allowed to have jobs, to have families or to participate fully in their communities.

As a result, spaces and places often do not work for disabled people.

We have stairs instead of ramps, buildings that aren't accessible and train stations that are hard to get around. As a result, some people are excluded from entire areas of their villages, towns or cities.

It's up to ALL OF US to make sure our world is MORE ACCESSIBLE.

It's our job to make sure that people with disabilities are treated with RESPECT.

Books are printed with letters that are too small, and subtitles don't appear automatically on films or TV shows.

We have sounds that are too loud, places that are too full of clamour and a world that can feel overwhelming for neurodiverse people.

As a result, neurodiverse people sometimes have to hide, or "mask", their disabilities in order to fit in and be able to live in the world that wasn't designed for them.

It's our job to make sure that people with disabilities are treated fairly.

It's up to all of us to WORK TOGETHER and make sure everyone FEELS WELCOME and at home in OUR WORLD.

A disability often limits what a person can do. This is called a **limitation**.

We often hear that anyone can do anything they set their mind to, but that is not always true. We all have limitations.

"I struggle with balance, and I need a cane."

"I take breaks from my computer due to my light sensitivity."

"I find reading hard, so I listen to audiobooks."

Learning to accept our own limitations can be tricky, but it is also one of the best gifts we can give ourselves.

We should always take care to respect our own limitations and the limitations of others.

NOT EVERYONE CAN DO EVERYTHING, AND THAT'S OK!

"I can't speak, but I love to dance with my brother."

"I get tired quickly, so my friend comes to my house to play."

"I need someone to push my wheelchair for me."

"I'm autistic and need comfort when I'm stressed."

It is WRONG to pick on someone because they are different.

NO ONE should ever tease or belittle someone else for something they can't do.

NO ONE should ever use their words or their actions to make someone else feel small.

It is WRONG to be unkind to someone because they have a disability.

It is WRONG to be ableist.

ABLEISM IS WRONG.

You might hear someone saying ableist things to you, or you might notice someone behaving in an ableist way towards someone else. If you do, tell an adult you trust.

IT IS OK TO BE PROUD OF BEING DIFFERENT!

AND IT IS OK TO BE CONFIDENT IN BEING DISABLED!

BEING AWARE, CONSIDERATE AND RESPECTFUL IS ALWAYS GOOD!

Being helpful to others requires **thoughtfulness**.

It is OK to ask a disabled person if they need help, but it is always up to them. Listen to them. They know best about their body – they know their body and mind better than anyone.

If someone says "no, thank you" to your offer of help, it is important to respect their answer. Sometimes, when well-meaning people try to help, they end up hurting instead.

If someone has a hard time communicating, it is never helpful to rush them or talk over them. Let them take their time to speak or make a point. It is important to allow people to communicate at their own pace and in their own way.

Many people use a mobility aid, such as a cane, a wheelchair or a walker. A person's mobility aid is an extension of them. Moving or touching their mobility aid without their permission is not helpful and should never be done.

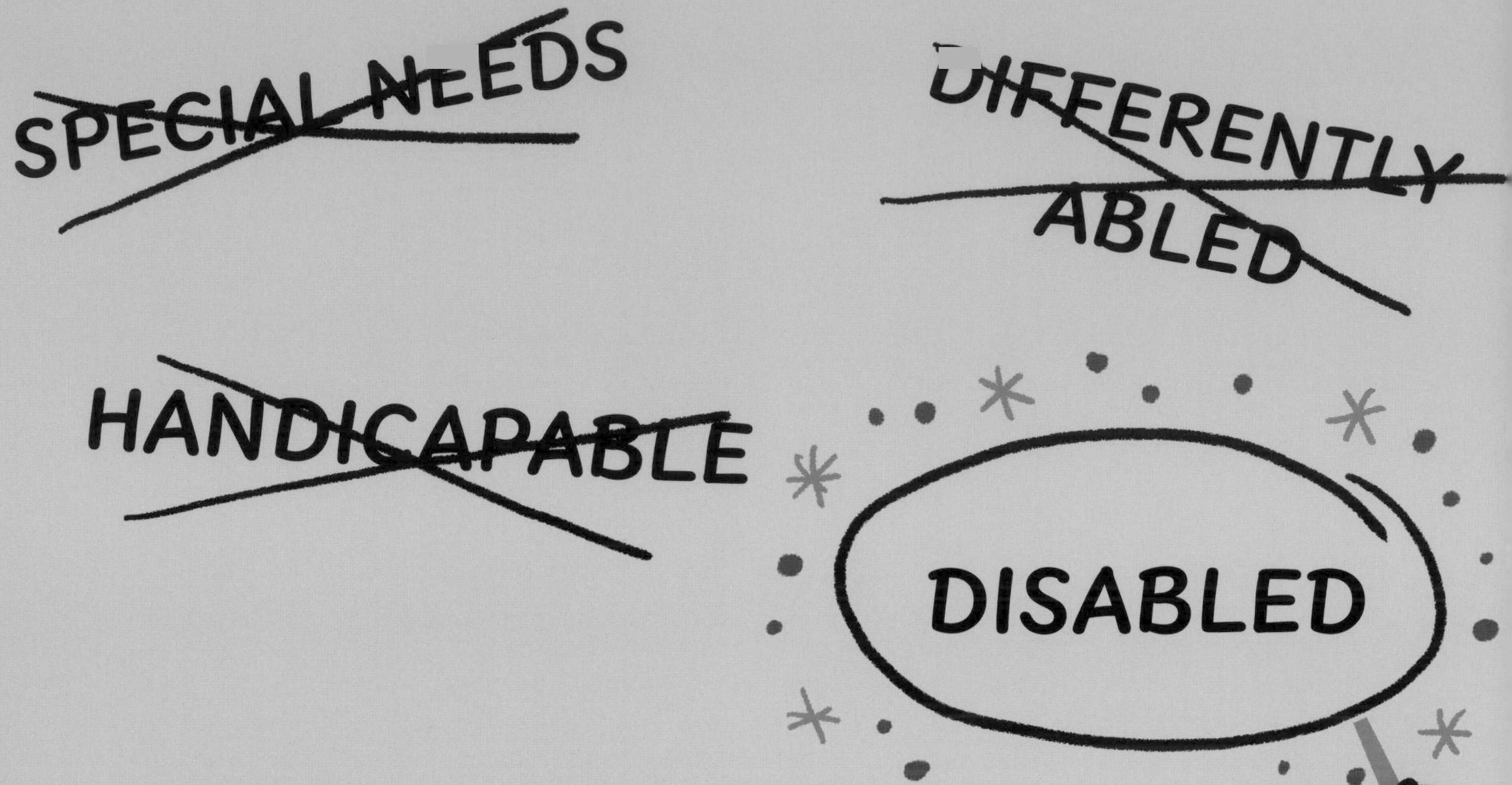

~~SPECIAL NEEDS~~

~~DIFFERENTLY ABLED~~

~~HANDICAPABLE~~

(DISABLED)

Disability is not a bad word.
There is nothing wrong with saying someone has a disability or is disabled. Disability is nothing to be ashamed of.

People with disabilities don't have "special needs". They have human needs, just like everyone else.

People aren't "handicapable", "handicapped" or "differently abled". They're disabled, and we don't need to make up other words or phrases!

Saying the word **disability** shouldn't make us uncomfortable, because disability is nothing to be uncomfortable about.

When we can, we should always ask someone how they would like to be described and do our best to respect their choice.

People with disabilities can do all sorts of things. They can write books, climb mountains, make beautiful art, lead businesses and compete in marathons.

Disabled people aren't inspiring just because they are living their everyday lives.

Disabled people constantly have to adapt to a world that is not made for them. In the future, we ought to have a more accessible world to look forward to.

A WORLD THAT IS NOT ABLEIST ENCOURAGES DISABLED PEOPLE TO SPEAK UP.

Adaptation and innovation can lead to things that benefit not only people with disabilities, but everyone else, too. We can have better and more accessible transportation, more flexible and welcoming jobs and schools, and cool new technologies.

The world is more virtual now than it has ever been before. We can speak to our friends and teachers online, and some adults can go to work from the comfort of their own homes! A virtual world means more access for everyone.

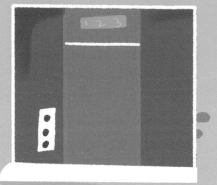

We have computers and phones that can turn our speech into text or our text into speech, virtual-reality headsets that can take us anywhere in this world or another and cars that drive themselves.

A WORLD THAT IS INCLUSIVE ENCOURAGES PEOPLE WITH DISABILITIES TO SHARE THEIR STORIES.

The future is bright!

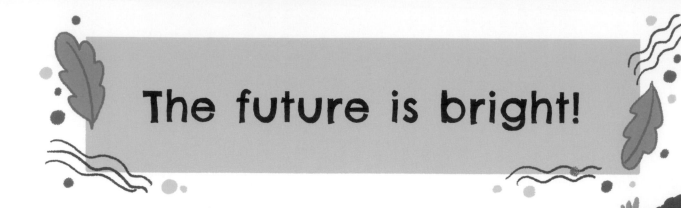

People being different from one another creates a richer, more vibrant society. Like anyone else, disabled people have many talents, skills and stories to share.

Like everyone else, disabled people deserve to tell their own stories. We can learn so much from each other's differences.

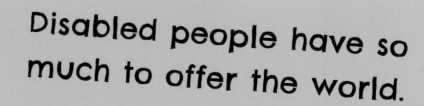
Disabled people have so much to offer the world.

Glossary

ableism: when people with disabilities are treated differently, poorly or unfairly because they are disabled

accessibility: everyone being able to use the things in the world around them, which is made easier in buildings that have lifts, buses that have wheelchair ramps, movies that have subtitles, news bulletins that feature sign language, and beyond

adapt: when you make changes to suit you and your needs

adaptation: a tool or way of doing something that allows you to adapt

coordination: the way that the brain, muscles and body parts work together to create movement

differences: the ways in which people and/or things are not the same

disability: a condition that can limit a person's ability to do something in a typical way, or at all; an ingenious and creative way to live in the world

disabled: a word used to describe someone who lives with a disability

diversity: all the ways in which we are different from one another, including our races, genders, religions, ethnicities, ages, cultures or disabilities

dynamic: a disability that is constantly changing

inclusive: welcoming of everyone

innovation: a new idea, thing or way of doing something

limitation: when a person's body or brain does not allow them to do something

mobility aid: an object or vehicle that offers its user more freedom, for example, crutches, a scooter and a wheelchair

neurodivergent: to have a brain that is different from a neurotypical brain, but equally as valuable. Autism and ADHD (attention deficit hyperactivity disorder) are examples of neurodiversity.

prosthetic: an artificial body part, such as a leg or ear

stim: repeated movement of the body, or a body part, such as hand flapping, finger clicking or eye blinking

Questions

Here are some questions to help prompt honest and open conversations around disability with friends and family.

How do films, TV shows and books portray disabled people and their lives?

Is it always the responsibility of someone with a disability to teach us about disability?

Is your home, school or community accessible? What could make it more so?

A note for adults reading this book

I Am, You Are is intended to start conversations around disability. I find that most true learning happens through honest and open conversations. Disability is an incredibly nuanced topic, and I know that there are ways in which this book may fall short of addressing all of these nuances, but I hope it will encourage the conversations that need to happen.

Authentic and accurate representation is critically important for children. It is crucial that disability is normalized for all children, and that it shows up naturally in their worlds of learning and play. It is especially important that disabled children get to see themselves reflected in the world around them.

Children are naturally curious. They tend to ask questions, but disabled people are not human search engines. We do not owe the world our private, personal information. It is the job of the adults in a child's life to provide disability representation in their home and learning environments. If disability is a regular part of a child's world, they will likely feel less of a need to ask personal or invasive questions of the disabled people they meet.

Providing children with accurate and thoughtful disability representation also means seeking out this representation for yourself. There is a wealth of resources created by disabled people for your consumption, benefit and betterment, including books, media, films, podcasts and the like.

Listen to disabled people and hear our stories. We have so much to offer the world.

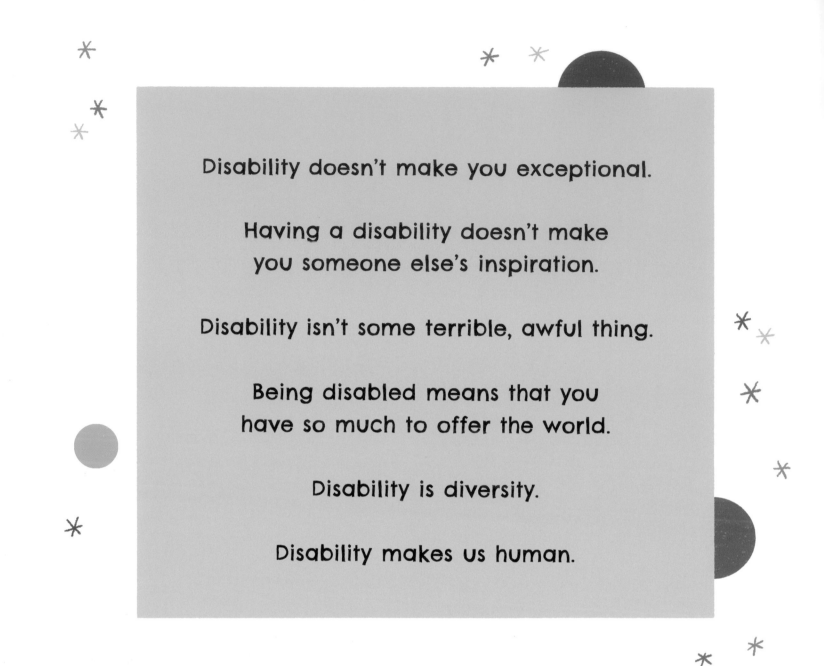

Disability doesn't make you exceptional.

Having a disability doesn't make
you someone else's inspiration.

Disability isn't some terrible, awful thing.

Being disabled means that you
have so much to offer the world.

Disability is diversity.

Disability makes us human.

Ashley Harris Whaley is a disabled writer, speaker, speech-language pathologist and activist. She works with the Cerebral Palsy Foundation and is the creator of Disability Reframed, a platform that focuses on changing perspectives through education and conversation. Ashley is a passionate public speaker who regularly educates on anti-ableism, disability identity, the language used around disability and allyship. Ashley's writing has appeared in Refinery29. *I Am, You Are* is her first book. She lives in North Carolina, USA, with her husband and pets. She owns way too many pairs of shoes that she can't actually walk in. Connect with her @disabilityreframed and @ashleyharriswhaley.

Ananya Rao-Middleton is an illustrator and disability activist who uses her work as a tool to speak truth to the voices of marginalized communities at the intersections of disability, gender, race and other oppressive systems. She is passionate about illustration as a way to "do" activism and has created artwork for Twitter, Refinery29, Instagram and the UK Parliament. Ananya lives in Lisbon, Portugal, where the sunshine is good for her multiple sclerosis and post-concussion syndrome. Keep in touch with Ananya @AnanyaPaints.

Hannah Wood is an illustrator of children's books. She was born in England but spent much of her childhood in the Netherlands and Norway. She now lives in a quaint little village in the middle of England with her two cats. Hannah supported Ananya with the illustrations for this book.